WELCOME TO THE WORLD OF
Beavers

Diane Swanson

Whitecap Books
Vancouver / Toronto

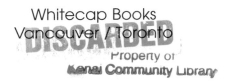

Edited by Elizabeth McLean
Cover design by Steve Penner
Interior design by Margaret Ng
Typeset by Jennifer Conroy
Photo credits: Tim Christie iv, 16; M. Quinton/First Light 2; Thomas
Kitchin/First Light 4, 14, 22, 24; Wayne Wegner/First Light 6, 12, 26;
Robert Lankinen/First Light 8; Michael Wheatley 10; Wayne Lynch 18, 20

Printed and bound in Canada

Canadian Cataloguing in Publication Data

Swanson, Diane, 1944–
    Welcome to the world of beavers

    Includes index.
    ISBN 1-55110-853-4

    1. Beavers—Juvenile literature. I. Title.
QL737.R63S92 1999   j599.37   C98-911025-7

For more information on
this series and other
Whitecap Books titles,
visit our web site at
www.whitecap.ca

The publisher acknowledges the support of the Canada Council for the Arts
and the Cultural Services Branch of the Government of British Columbia for
our publishing program. We acknowledge the financial support of the
Government of Canada through the Book Industry Development Program
for our publishing activities.

The author gratefully acknowledges the support of the British Columbia
Arts Council.

Contents

World of Difference

With sharp teeth for tools, a beaver can easily cut down trees.

THE BITE OF A BEAVER CAN TOPPLE TALL TREES. Using strong jaw muscles, the beaver can chomp through a trunk more than half a metre (1 ½ feet) thick. Its four front teeth—an upper and lower pair—are built for gnawing. They're long and strong, and as sharp as chisels. They're always growing, and they never get dull. These amazing teeth are even protected from chipping by a hard orange coating.

Beavers are rodents—animals that have four special teeth for gnawing. The rodent family includes mice, squirrels, and porcupines. In North America, the beaver

1

Beavers are well known for their dense fur and broad tails.

is the biggest member of this family. It can weigh as much as a large dog and measure 1 metre (about 3 feet) long, including its tail.

Thick beaver coats range in color from yellow-brown to reddish to almost black. They're made of two different kinds of fur: long and silky, and short and woolly. The coats are always kept clean and well oiled, which helps beavers stay dry.

The wide, flat tail of a beaver has very little hair. Instead, it's covered with thick, leathery scales. A scaly tail is easier to flip around in water. It moves like a rudder—up, down, or side to side—whenever the beaver swims.

Don't let the little eyes, ears, and nostrils of a beaver fool you. It can see well both above and below water. Its hearing is excellent, and its sense of smell is super keen.

BEAVER GIANTS

Thousands—even millions—of years ago, beavers grew as big as bears. Some were more than 2.5 metres (8 feet) long and weighed 360 kilograms (800 pounds). Along with mammoths and other giants of their time, these beavers lived in Europe, Asia, and North America. Scientists think they fed on plants that grew in marshes. Some native North Americans believed that giant beavers built continents by scooping up mud and stones from an ancient sea.

3

Where in the World

BEAVERS ARE AT HOME IN WATER CLOSE TO WOODS. When they look for places to settle, they often head for lakes, ponds, or lazy streams with plenty of trees nearby.

Water helps protect beavers. On their stubby legs, they can't easily escape fast-running enemies such as wolves and bears. But beavers can swim fast. By building their homes in the water or along the banks, they're never far from safety.

Woods grow most of the food beavers need—especially tree bark. They also provide the branches and twigs that beavers

Heading home to its pond, this beaver feels safest in the water.

5

Swimming over a dam is no challenge for a water expert like the beaver.

use to build homes, called lodges, in the water. If they dig out a den in a bank instead, they might use tree branches and twigs to cover it.

A family of beavers needs quite a large area, or territory. They may claim a stretch of shoreline up to 2 kilometres (more than a mile) long. When young beavers grow up, they travel at least 50 kilometres (30 miles) to find places of their own. Some have moved as far as 250 kilometres (150 miles).

In North America, beavers live from the Arctic to Mexico and from the Pacific Ocean to the Atlantic. By swimming through salt water, they have even settled on many of the islands that lie along both coasts. Some beavers also live in a few parts of Europe and Asia. Although they are less common today, their numbers are still healthy.

Strong, graceful swimmers, beavers are champions in the water. They can speed along at 8 kilometres (5 miles) an hour. Their broad, webbed back feet provide the power, while their tails do most of the steering.

When beavers dive, they close their ears and nostrils. See-through lids protect their eyes. Flaps of skin behind their big front teeth keep water out of their mouths. Beavers can stay underwater for up to 15 minutes at a time.

World of the Builder

LEAVE IT TO BEAVERS TO BUILD A GREAT HOME. They might first raise a dam, creating a deep pond that won't freeze to the bottom in winter. The dam might also widen the pond and make nearby trees even easier to reach.

Beavers start building by poking sticks into the mud beneath the water. Layer by layer, they add twigs, branches, and rocks. They also use any empty bottles or old tires that they find. Carrying, dragging, rolling, or floating their building materials, the beavers work hard to get them to the dam site.

Finally, they scoop up mud with their

Fresh mud is great for filling cracks in a beaver lodge.

9

Even in snowy winters, beavers keep warm inside their lodge.

handlike front paws and pack it into the cracks. A finished dam can be more than 5 metres (16 feet) tall. The beavers work to keep it leakproof all year round.

In the middle of the pond, beavers might build a lodge in much the same way. Big families make big lodges, but most are about 5 metres (16 feet) wide. They often rise about 2 metres (6.5 feet) above the water.

The beavers make under-water openings in the lodge. Then they cut out one or more rooms above the water surface for gathering, eating, and sleeping. Often they blanket the floor of a sleeping area with soft layers of shredded wood.

Fresh air enters through openings in the roof. Beavers heat the lodge with their own bodies. You'll know they're at home if you spot warm air rising from the roof on a cold day.

HOME IMPROVEMENT

Beaver dams help make good homes for many animals besides beavers. Fish and frogs move into ponds that the dams create. Mink and muskrat settle along the shore. Birds and bats skim across the water. Moose wade in to feed.

Many new plants grow where beavers have cut down trees, providing food for rabbits and deer. Even trees that die from the flooding caused by beavers become homes for raccoons and woodpeckers.

World Full of Food

A HUNGRY BEAVER IS A BUSY BEAVER. It has to gnaw trees to get its favorite food. Working mostly at night, the beaver chisels its way through a trunk, then scrambles aside to avoid the falling tree. The best parts to eat are the bark, twigs, buds, and leaves.

Beavers prefer aspen, poplar, willow, and birch trees, but they also eat other kinds of trees, including cherry and apple. Luckily for the beaver, it can use the same trees for eating as it does for building. After it strips branches and small trunks bare, it can add them to a lodge or dam.

Crack! Snap! Twigs make a fast but healthy meal.

13

Too hungry to wait, this beaver chows down before it gets home.

As beavers chew down trees close to the water, they must head farther away for food. To make the job easier, they dig deep canals that may be wider than your bed and hundreds of metres (several hundreds of feet) long. Water from a pond, lake, or river flows through the canals, and beavers float logs and branches along them.

Summer provides easy-to-get treats for beavers. They nibble on grasses, berries, flowers, and most kinds of water plants. And they can be very tidy snackers. When beavers eat thick lily pads, for example, they first roll them up like tubes. They hold food in their front paws—much like you do in your hands.

Sometimes there's not enough food around—even for hard-working beavers. But they're prepared for tough times. They can use energy from fat stored in their tails.

FOOD FROM THE ICEBOX

Each fall, northern beavers pack away food for the winter. They choose a spot in deep water close to home and pile up layers of branches. Through the winter, they visit this "icebox" whenever they need food.

Beavers may also swim just beneath the ice to grab roots of cattails and other water plants. On mild days, they sometimes leave the water to eat. By climbing on top of deep snow, they can often chew the bark high up on tall trees.

15

World of Words

A TAIL SLAP CAN SOUND LIKE A GUN SHOT—if the tail belongs to a beaver. When they sense danger, beavers often whack their tails hard on the water. The sound can travel 2 kilometres (more than a mile), warning other beavers and sometimes scaring off enemies such as coyotes.

Tail talk is loud, but it's not the only talking beavers do. Young beavers—called kits—squeal softly to welcome their mothers back home. They also whine and coo in high-pitched voices, but when they want food, they g-rr-unt.

Beavers often talk to their kits by

"Let's get out of here!" A beaver sounds the alarm by slapping the water with its tail.

17

The beaver has a nose for news. It smells messages left by other beavers.

rubbing noses and making noises. All family members talk while they're cleaning themselves. It's a gentle, comforting sound.

Beavers also talk by setting out smelly signs. Around their territory, they pile up mud and bits of plants—sometimes on top of stones. The piles may be 35 centimetres (14 inches) tall. The beavers wet them with smelly oils from glands at their back ends.

By sniffing signs, a beaver can tell if they were made by members of its family or not. It also knows whether the sign makers are male or female, young or old. If a male finds the smelly sign of a male from another family, he may drive the outsider away by hissing, growling, and slapping his tail. But if he discovers the signs of a female from another family, he may follow them to find her. She just might become his mate.

LOOKING GOOD, FEELING BETTER

Beavers have handy combs: the claws on all four feet. They comb their thick fur often to remove matts, dirt, and burrs. One claw on each of their back feet is split. It helps the beavers waterproof their fur, spreading oil from glands at their back ends and at the roots of their hair.

Tucked away in their dry lodges or dens, beavers often comb one another. It not only helps keep their fur in good shape, it seems to relax the beavers.

New World

MATES FOR NOW, MATES FOREVER.
Most beavers choose their partners for life.
Together, they build their homes, defend
their territories, and raise their families.

In spring, a beaver gives birth in her
lodge or den to three or four kits. Each one
is only as long as a pen and weighs about as
much as a loaf of bread.

Newborn beavers are amazing. They
already have teeth and furry beaver coats.
They can see, and they can walk. Within a
few days, kits can even swim, but they don't
go past the water just below their home.

Snuggling and snoozing, the young

Peek inside a
beaver lodge and
you might spot
a mother with
her kit.

Father beaver hurries home with a fresh branch for his family's lunch.

kits spend most of their time near their mother. She keeps them safe and warm, and she feeds them her milk—up to nine times a day. Gradually, she adds tender twigs to their meals. Their father usually gathers and delivers the food.

The parents also work to keep the kits' bed clean. Every one or two days, they dump the old layer of wood chips or grass in the water and replace it with fresh bedding.

Kits may be only four days old when they start to clean themselves. Still, their parents help them care for their fur.

If a beaver mother must leave her kits, older siblings often babysit. Beaver families usually include three or four beavers that are one to two years old. Like their parents, these sitters are quick to rescue a kit that tumbles into the water. They often haul it back by the tail.

CLOSE ROOMMATES

In North America, another animal also begins life in a beaver lodge. A beaver beetle—smaller than this "o"—lays its eggs on the floor. When the eggs hatch, the beetles move onto a resting beaver. Tiny hooks and combs on their bodies help them cling to their furry host.

Beaver beetles spend almost all of their lives on a beaver. They feed by scraping their host's skin and dining on the oil in it. They don't seem to bother the beaver much.

Small World

WHEN IT'S TIME TO EXPLORE, KITS TAKE TO THE WATER. They cling to one of their parents until they're heavy enough to practice diving. That's a skill they need to reach the underwater openings to their home.

At first, a parent beaver coaches its kits, swimming along beside them. If they tire, they can always get help. Some parents use their mouths to hold and push the kits. Others give them piggyback rides home.

Kits usually complete their diving lessons in one or two nights. Then they're ready to follow older beavers around, watching and

Staying close to its mother, a young beaver learns to carry food through the water.

25

Young beavers like to play. What game might these three be up to?

imitating what they do. The kits practice being beavers by gnawing trees and digging canals.

By fall, some kits start to help their families gather and store food underwater. Small kits may have to dive again and again before they can drag a branch down to the storage pile. It can take a full year for kits to become skilled at cutting trees and building dams.

As busy as beavers are, their life is not all work. Sometimes they float lazily down a stream on their backs, or they chase one another around, like children playing tag. Beavers of all ages seem to like swooping up and down in the water, occasionally leaping over other beavers.

By age two, most beavers are ready to leave home and start their own families. They have about 10 years of busy living ahead of them yet.

BUSY, BUSY BEAVERS

Beavers often amaze people. Here are just some of the reasons why:

- A beaver dam can be as long as 1500 metres (4900 feet). Some dams are strong enough for a horse to cross.
- When beavers gnaw down trees, they often prop themselves up on their tails.
- A pair of beavers can build a small dam in 24 hours.
- Beavers can cut down trees more than 30 metres (100 feet) tall.

27

Index